Pro
for S
Days

Illustrated by Jill Barklem

LITTLE LIONS

Sunday

For this new Sunday with its light,
For rest and shelter of the night,
We thank you, heavenly Father.
Through this new week but just begun,
Be near, and help us every one
To please you, heavenly Father.

A Happy Day

Thank you for each happy day,
For fun, for friends,
and work and play;
Thank you for your loving care,
Here at home and everywhere.

Today

Dear Lord Jesus, we shall have
this day only once; before it is
gone, help us to do all the
good we can, so that today is
not a wasted day.

My Birthday

O loving God, today is my birthday. For your care from the day I was born until today and for your love, I thank you. Help me to be strong and healthy, and to show love for others, as Jesus did.

Autumn Days

All good gifts around us
Are sent from heaven above;
Then thank the Lord,
  O thank the Lord,
For all his love.

Thank you, our heavenly Father for harvest time: for ripe fruit in the orchards and berries in the hedges: for the vegetable harvest and all the food gathered in and stored for winter days.

A Spoilt Day

O God, you made us and you love us, thank you for being so willing to forgive us. Make us quick to own up to you whenever we do wrong, so that we may quickly be forgiven. Then our day will not be spoilt by worry and we can be happy all day long, through Jesus Christ our Lord.

Days when we are ill

You're marvellous, God, loving
everyone the way you do.
I don't like having to stay in
bed but when I talk to you I
know you love me and that's
great. Some children always
have to stay in bed and never
get out to make friends. Love
them too, and help them.
Loving everyone is difficult.
I can't do it but you can
manage it, God. Perhaps I'd
better try and learn. Teach me
now while I'm ill and there's
plenty of time.

Lord Jesus, I am ill.
Please make me well.
Help me to be brave,
and thankful to the people
looking after me.
Thank you for being here with me.

Holidays

Loving Father, on this day
Make us happy in our play,
Kind and helpful, playing fair,
Letting others have a share.

Thank you, God, for holidays
In the lovely summer days,
For our picnics, for our fun,
For our playing in the sun.
Make us good, with smiling faces,
So our homes are friendly places,
And the helpful things we do
Make all our mothers happy too.

Copyright ©1978 Lion Publishing

Published by
Lion Publishing plc
Icknield Way, Tring, Herts, England
ISBN 0 85648 112 2
Lion Publishing Corporation
10885 Textile Road, Belleville, Michigan 48111, USA
ISBN 0 85648 112 2
Albatross Books Pty Ltd
PO Box 320, Sutherland, NSW 2232, Australia
ISBN 0 86760 302 X

First edition 1978
Reprinted 1979, 1981, 1983, 1984, 1985, 1986

Printed and bound in Italy

Acknowledgments
'For this new Sunday with its light' from *A Brownie Guide Prayer Book* by
Rosalie Wakefield, SPCK. 'O Loving God' from *Children's Prayers from
Other Lands*, Curtis Brown Ltd. 'Thank you, our heavenly Father' from
Ladybird Book of Prayers Through the Year by H. I. Rostron, Ladybird
Books Ltd. 'O God, you made us' from *Prayers for Today's Church* by
Dick Williams, Church Pastoral-Aid Society. 'You're marvellous, God' from
Prayabout, Church Information Office. 'Lord Jesus, I am ill' by Zinnia
Bryan from *Let's Talk to God Again*, Scripture Union. 'Loving Father, on
this day' by D. M. Prescott from *The Infant Teacher's Prayer Book*,
Blandford Press. 'Thank you, God, for holidays' by Irene Taylor and
Phyllis Garlick from *All Our Days*, Church Missionary Society